Bible Studies
for Soul Winners

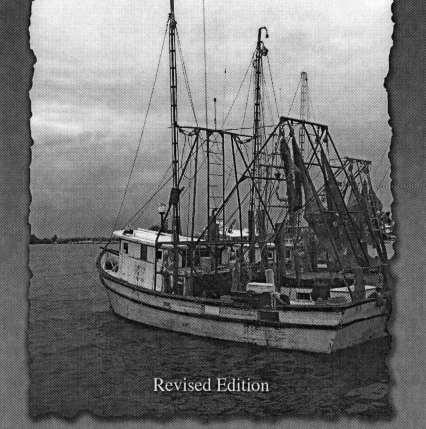

Revised Edition

Nate Krupp

"Making ready a
people for the Lord."
Luke 1:17

2121 Barnes Avenue SE · Salem, OR 97306 USA

Scripture quotations are taken from the New American Standard
translation (hereafter NASB) unless otherwise indicated.

Preparing the Way Publishers edition 2004

Copyright ©1962
by Nate Krupp

Over 30,000 copies in print

Published by

2121 Barnes Avenue SE
Salem, OR 97306 USA

Permission to translate this book in its entirety into other languages will be
granted by the author upon request to: Nate Krupp, 2121 Barnes Avenue
SE, Salem, OR 97306, USA; telephone 503-585-4054, fax 503-375-8401,
email kruppnj@open.org

Cover photography and design: Clint Crittenden

ISBN 1-929451-17-2
Library of Congress Control Number 2004092622

Printed in the United States of America

Contents

Introduction 5

Bible Study 1 – Sin and its Consequences 7

Bible Study 2 – God's Remedy for Sin 11

Bible Study 3 – Man's Response 15

Bible Study 4 – Our Task of Evangelism 19

Bible Study 5 – God's Part in Evangelism 23

Bible Study 6 – Man's Part in Evangelism (1) 29

Bible Study 7 – Man's Part in Evangelism (2) 33

Bible Study 8 – Jesus' Evangelism 37

Bible Study 9 – The First Century Church's Evangelism 43

Conclusion 49

Other Helpful Materials from PTWP 50

Introduction

The Lord Jesus Christ gave one central task to His followers—to communicate the gospel to every person in the world in every generation (Mark 16:15). This Bible study series is written for the Christian who desires to know and do his part in seeing this task accomplished. It will give you a thorough, biblical understanding of evangelism and motivate you for soul winning.

These studies can be used in daily devotions or family worship; discussed in mid-week prayer meeting; or used as a study guide for men's, women's, and youth group meetings, and at conventions, seminars, and retreats on soul winning. And it can be the basis of part of a course on evangelism at Bible schools, Christian colleges, and seminaries.

The following suggestions are given for its most effective use:

FOR INDIVIDUAL STUDY

1. Use this booklet as a study aid along with your Bible.
2. Do one study each week, spending about 15 minutes each day.
3. First read the study introduction. Give special thought to the question(s) asked therein.
4. Next, do the study questions, just a few each day. Read the question, find the answer by turning to the Bible reference(s) given, and write the answer in the blank(s) in your own words. You may wish to consult several translations.
5. As you do the study, ask the Holy Spirit to begin to show you a specific way or ways that you should **apply** the truths of the study to your own life. Then, when you have finished all the questions, write a **detailed application** of exactly how you are going to apply one specific truth.
6. You are strongly encouraged to memorize the verses suggested at the end of each chapter.

FOR GROUP STUDY

The individuals in the group should do the studies on their own during the week as suggested above. The group then will meet for about an hour once each week to share study results and applications, to quote memorized verses to one another, and to pray for unsaved friends. A leader for each meeting should guide, but not monopolize, the discussion.

Sin and Its Consequences

INTRODUCING THE TRUTH

When one looks at the prayerlessness, the busyness about things of secondary importance, and the appalling unconcern for lost souls which is the pattern of many evangelical Christians and churches today, it is wondered how much we truly believe in the reality and terrible consequences of sin.

Shouldn't a real look at the terrible consequences of sin in this life and in the next break our hearts for a lost world? Seeing what God has to say about man's need of salvation is the place to start in becoming a more effective soul winner. Meditate on the truths of this study, and ask God to fill your heart with compassion for a world that is lost.

FINDING THE TRUTH

1. What is it which makes salvation a necessity for every person?

   Romans 3:9-12, 23 _____

   _____

   _____

   _____

2. Who brought this problem of sin into the world? Romans 5:12,

   1 Corinthians 15:22 _____

   _____

   _____

   _____

3. Why has every person since Adam had this same problem?

   Psalm 51:5, Ephesians 2:3 _____

   _____

   _____

   _____

4. What are some ways that man sins?

   1 John 3:4 _____

   _____

   Romans 14:23_____

   _____

   James 4:17 _____

   _____

5. What is the consequence or result of sin? Romans 6:23, Ezekiel

   18:4 _____

   _____

6. In what life does this death begin? Ephesians 2:1, 1 Timothy 5:6

   _____

   _____

   _____

7. Under whose power does sinful man live? Acts 26:18 _____

   _____

   _____

   _____

8. What has he done to those under his power? 2 Corinthians 4:3-4

_____

_____

_____

9. To what can people without Christ be compared? Matthew 9:36,

1 Peter 2:25 _____

_____

_____

_____

10. What is God's attitude toward sinful man? Romans 1:18, John

3:36 _____

_____

_____

11. What is sinful man's destination? Matthew 11:23, Luke 16:23

_____

_____

_____

12. Who else will be there? Matthew 25:41 _____

_____

_____

_____

13. What will it be like there? Mark 9:47-48, Matthew 22:13 _____

_____

_____

_____

14. What will occur to sinful man in his final destination?

    2 Thessalonians 1:9 _____

_____

_____

15. How long will existence in this final state last? Matthew 25:41,46

_____

_____

APPLYING THE TRUTH

_____

_____

_____

_____

_____

_____

_____

_____

MEMORIZING THE TRUTH – Romans 3:23, Romans 6:23

Bible Study Two

God's Remedy for Sin

INTRODUCING THE TRUTH

How wonderful it is, after considering the terribleness of sin, to know that there is another side to the picture. God has provided a way of reconciliation. A remedy for sin has been made. Man can be saved. Man need not spend eternity in hell. And he can actually experience a life of fellowship with God in this life.

Should not a fresh glimpse of God and His infinite love for lost humanity compel us to go into the streets and lanes of the city to proclaim to lost men this wonderful Good News?

FINDING THE TRUTH

1. What provision has God made for sinful man? Romans 6:23

_____

_____

_____

2. Why has God done this? John 3:16 _____

_____

_____

_____

3. What is the visible proof of God's love? 1 John 4:10_____

_____

_____

_____

4. In whom is eternal life or salvation found? John 14:6, Romans

    6:23 _____

    _____

5. Why is it in or through Jesus Christ? Romans 5:8 _____

    _____

    _____

    _____

6. What did the death of Christ on the cross accomplish? Ephesians

    2:13-16, Colossians 1:20-22 _____

    _____

    _____

    _____

    _____

    _____

7. How? 1 Peter 3:18, Hebrews 9:28 _____

    _____

    _____

    _____

8. What happens to man's sins when he is saved? Acts 3:19, Psalm

    103:12 _____

    _____

    _____

    _____

9. Is there any other way of salvation? Acts 4:12 _____

_____

_____

_____

10. What is God's provision called? Mark 13:10, Romans 1:16

_____

_____

_____

11. Is there any way that man can earn this salvation? Ephesians 2:8-9,

Titus 3:5 _____

_____

_____

_____

12. Whom does God want to see saved? 2 Peter 3:9, 1 Timothy 2:3-4

_____

_____

_____

13. As an unsaved person responds to the gospel, what are some of

the things which God does in and for him?

Acts 3:19, 1 John 1:9 _____

_____

John 3:3-7, 1 Peter 1:23 _____

_____

Romans 8:9, 1 Corinthians 3:16 _____

_____

Romans 8:16, Galatians 4:6 _____

_____

Ephesians 2:5, Colossians 2:13 _____

_____

2 Corinthians 5:17, Galatians 6:15 _____

_____

1 John 3:9, 1 Corinthians 10:13 _____

_____

APPLYING THE TRUTH

_____
_____
_____
_____
_____
_____
_____
_____
_____
_____

MEMORIZING THE TRUTH – John 3:16, Romans 5:8

Bible Study Three

Man's Response

INTRODUCING THE TRUTH

God has provided man with a wonderful way of salvation. Now what? Is there something man must do in response to God's provision? And if so, what? And how?

As soul winners we must know what men must do to be saved and then help them to do it. So let's further equip ourselves for our task of fishing for men by seeing what is involved.

FINDING THE TRUTH

1. What must man do before he can begin to respond to God's offered gift of salvation? Romans 10:17, John 5:24 *It takes faith 3. believing 3 listening*

2. Does salvation come to one automatically or is it to be sought? Acts 16:29-30, Romans 10:13 *You have to ask 3. seek to get it*

3. What must man's attitude toward his life of sin be as he responds to the gospel? Luke 13:3, Acts 3:19 *Be willing to repent 3 turn from life of sin. Walk away from temptation.*

Bible Studies for Soul Winners

4. What does it mean to repent? Isaiah 55:7 _to turn_
from sinful ways _____

_____

5. What must man then do to be saved? Acts 16:31, John 3:16____
Believe in the Lord Jesus that
He died for you & you will be
saved

6. What does true belief in Christ involve? John 1:12 _____
Receiving him & believing him

_____

Revelation 3:20 _Opening the door to Him_

_____

7. In what way do many people take this step of faith in Christ?
Romans 10:13 _everyone who calls on_
the name of the Lord will be
saved.

8. How does one who has put his faith in Christ become related to
God? John 1:12, Romans 8:16 _The Spirit bears_
witness with our spirit that
we are children of God. By
believing in Him we have a
right to become children w/ God.

9. Of what kingdom does he become a part? Luke 8:1, Colossians 1:13 _The kingdom of God, the kingdom of the Son He loves_

10. What should one who has taken this step of faith do?

    Matthew 10:32-33, Romans 10:9-10 _Acknowledge Jesus Christ_

    Leviticus 6:4, Luke 19:8-9 _realize his guilt & seek restoration._

    Acts 2:38, Acts 8:36-38 _Repent & be baptized,_

11. Can a person know that he is saved? 1 John 5:11-13 _Whoever has the Son has life. Whoever does not have the Son, does not have life._

12. What are some of the evidences or proofs whereby one can know that he is saved? 1 John 3:9 _He who is born of God cannot keep sinning_

    1 John 5:4 _We get faith which gives us victory when we are born of God_

    1 John 3:14 _Love everyone_

13. What are some of the things that a person does as a result of his faith in Jesus Christ? Luke 9:23, Hebrews 5:9 Deny himself & take up His cross

Matthew 7:21, 1 John 2:17 Living for God, reading the Bible & learning how to live for Him

Ephesians 2:10, Titus 3:8 Do good works that He has for you to do

Matthew 24:13, Luke 9:62, Hebrews 12:1 endure til the end no looking back to the life of sin, lay aside sin

APPLYING THE TRUTH

MEMORIZING THE TRUTH – Acts 3:19, John 1:12

Bible Study Four

Our Task of Evangelism

INTRODUCING THE TRUTH

If the message of God's provision for sinful man demands a response on man's part, then the message, including the demanded response, must be communicated to lost men.

Whose job is it to do this communicating? What task has the Lord committed to His Church? And to just what extent is the Christian to be individually responsible and involved in this task? We wander aimlessly as ships without a rudder until we bring into clear focus the answers to these questions.

FINDING THE TRUTH

1. What has the Lord committed to His followers? 1 Corinthians 9:16-17, 1 Thessalonians 2:4 _to preach the gospel, speak to please God not man._

2. What are the Lord's followers to do with the gospel? Mark 16:15, 1 Corinthians 9:16 _preach the gospel to all creation_

3. To whom is the gospel to be taken? Mark 16:15 _every part of the world_

4. What are the four basic parts of this assignment?

Matthew 28:19-20 *Go, make disciples, baptize in the name of Father, Son, Holy Spirit, teach them to obey the commandments*

5. Upon what basis can the Lord make such an assignment?

Matthew 28:18 *His authority - all the authority*

6. Why is it so essential that this gospel be published to every creature? Romans 1:16 *So that everyone will understand*

7. What ministry, then, has been given to each of the Lord's followers? 2 Corinthians 5:18-19 *Reconciled to God - help people get right with God*

8. What then do the Lord's followers actually become?

2 Corinthians 5:20 *ambassadors for Christ we represent Christ*

word picture

OUR TASK OF EVANGELISM

9. Who is the center of this proclamation? Acts 1:8, Colossians 1:28

Christ and the holy spirit gives us power to proclaim his word

10. By what power is this work to be done? Luke 24:49, Acts 1:8

the holy spirit

11. In what manner are the Lord's followers to do their work?
John 20:21 Peacefully and we are to be doing the Lord's work

12. Where are the Lord's followers to begin in their task of evangelism? Luke 24:47, Acts 1:8 to all nations

13. What is the ultimate responsibility? Acts 1:8, Mark 16:15

To go into all the world and proclaim the gospel to all creation

APPLYING THE TRUTH

_____

_____

_____

_____

_____

_____

_____

_____

_____

_____

_____

_____

_____

_____

_____

_____

_____

_____

_____

MEMORIZING THE TRUTH – Mark 16:15, Acts 1:8

Bible Study Five

God's Part in Evangelism

INTRODUCING THE TRUTH

How utterly helpless we feel when we begin to catch a glimpse of the task of telling the gospel to every person in this generation unless we also see what God does. He prepares the Christian for the task of evangelism. And He prepares the unsaved to be receptive to the message.

All authority in heaven and in earth is given to the Lord Jesus, and all power and ability to prepare both harvest and harvester is the Holy Spirit's. What more do we need? What acceptable reason can we give for not having evangelized the world long ago?

FINDING THE TRUTH

1. What is the one thing that God does to prepare His people to do the work of evangelism? Ephesians 5:26, Hebrews 9:14 _____
   cleanses through the word, purifying our conscience

2. What are His instruments for doing this? Romans 15:16, 1 Peter 1:2 *sanctified by the Holy Spirit*
   Ephesians 5:26, John 15:3 *through the Word*

   1 John 1:7, Hebrews 9:14 *the blood of Jesus Christ*

3. What else does God do to prepare His people to witness and win souls? Luke 24:49, Acts 1:8 Wait until you're under the power of the Holy Spirit

4. How does He do this? Acts 4:8, 4:31, 13:9 through the Holy Spirit

5. What must the Christian watch in His Spirit-filled life? Ephesians 4:30 that he doesn't grieve the Holy Spirit

1 Thessalonians 5:19 Do not quench extenguish the Spirit or despise prophecies

6. What Divine teacher does the Christian have to further prepare him for the work of evangelism? John 14:26, 1 John 2:27 anointing of the holy spirit

7. Who is it that sends or commissions the Christian to work in the harvest? Matthew 9:38, Acts 13:4 the Lord's the holy spirit

GOD'S PART IN EVANGELISM

8. What is the Christian's weapon as he goes to conquer for Christ?
   Mark 4:14, Ephesians 6:17 _the Word_

   _____

9. What power does it have? Jeremiah 5:14 _fire & hammer_

   fire

   Jeremiah 23:29 _fire & hammer_

   _____

   Romans 1:16 _____

   _____

   Hebrews 4:12 _____

   _____

10. What has God promised regarding the use of His word? Isaiah
    55:11 _success_

    _____

    _____

11. What promise does Jesus give those who go to evangelize?
    Matthew 28:20, Hebrews 13:5-6 _He will never_
    leave you

12. What else has the Lord promised to do through those who evan-
    gelize for Him? Mark 16:17-18 _Cast out demons,_
    speak in new tongues, protection,
    healing

    _____

13. Additionally, what does the Lord do as His followers work at the task of evangelism? Mark 16:20 _accompanies them_

14. Who guides and directs a person doing the work of evangelism? Acts 8:29, 10:19 _the Spirit_

15. What does God do as the follower of the Lord, filled with the Spirit and armed with the Word of God, does the work of evangelism? John 16:8, Acts 24:25 _He will convict the world_

    John 15:26, John 8:18 _He will bear witness_

    Acts 16:14 _Opens their heart_

16. When we consider all that God does to prepare the way for evangelism, what should be our attitude toward the harvest? Joel 3:13, Matthew 9:37 _prepare for a big harvest_

    John 9:4, Luke 2:49 _We need to be winning souls now before we're out of time_

APPLYING THE TRUTH

_____

_____

_____

_____

_____

_____

_____

_____

_____

_____

_____

_____

_____

_____

_____

_____

_____

_____

_____

MEMORIZING THE TRUTH – Matthew 28:18, Luke 10:2

Bible Studies for Soul Winners

Bible Study Six

Man's Part in Evangelism (1)

INTRODUCING THE TRUTH

Getting the gospel to every person in the world in this generation is our task. Just how do we do this? How do we prepare ourselves for this work? And exactly how do we go about accomplishig the task?

Discovering these things will give us the foundation upon which we, as individual Christians, can build our lives and work for the Lord.

FINDING THE TRUTH

1. Who has God chosen to use in reaching a world lost in sin?

   2 Corinthians 5:20 _us - We are ambassadors for Christ_

2. What does the Lord want to make of His followers?

   Matthew 4:19 _fishers of men_

3. In doing this work of reconciliation, whose place does the soul winner take? 2 Corinthians 5:20 _Christ - we are doing his work_

4. What two-fold task is the Lord's follower chosen and ordained to do? John 15:16 ① *To go* ② *Bear fruit that will last & ask in His name*

5. What two things does one do when he brings forth fruit? John 15:8 *bear fruit & prove to be His disciples*

6. What is the soul winner to do before he goes? Luke 24:49, Ephesians 5:18 *filled w/ the spirit, waits stay & be*

7. With what is this associated? 2 Corinthians 7:1, 2 Timothy 2:21-22 *purifing, Perfecting ourself, holiness, honor, good work, righteousness, faith, love, peace*

8. What is to be a very real part of the soul winner's life? Luke 18:1, Matthew 18:19 *always pray & agree w/ each other in prayer never give up*

MAN'S PART IN EVANGELISM (1)

9. With what practice is this often associated? Matthew 6:16-18, Acts 14:23 *fasting*

10. What is to be another very real part of the life of a soul winner? Acts 17:11, 2 Timothy 2:15 *eagerness + examine scriptures daily, do best, great work*

11. What must the soul winner's attitude be toward self? Matthew 16:24-25, Mark 8:34-35 *must deny selves and take up cross + follow Christ*

12. What must his attitude be toward the things of this life? Matthew 6:19-21, 1 John 2:15-17 *store up treasures in heaven - not on earth, don't love the world - it will pass away + if we do, we don't have the Lord's love in us.*

13. What then must be done with self, possessions, and all that is a part of this life? Philippians 3:7-8, Romans 12:1 *It be considered garbage - Nothing matters when compared to Christ. Offer ourselves up to God.*

APPLYING THE TRUTH

_____

_____

_____

_____

_____

_____

_____

_____

_____

_____

_____

_____

_____

_____

_____

_____

_____

_____

_____

MEMORIZING THE TRUTH – John 15:16, Luke 14:33

Bible Study Seven

Man's Part in Evangelism (2)

INTRODUCING THE TRUTH

Preparing ourselves to be instruments that the Holy Spirit can use in His harvest is the first thing the Christian must do in fulfillment of his personal responsiblity for a lost world.

Then we must get at the job. Just exactly how do we go about this? What are the essential God-given requirements to be fulfilled in bringing people to Christ? Then what is our responsibility after they turn to Him? Let's see.

FINDING THE TRUTH

1. Whose example is the soul winner to follow as he does the work of evangelism? John 20:21 _Jesus_

   _____

   _____

2. Following the Lord's example, what is one of the first things one must do to reach an unsaved person for God? Luke 19:10 ____
   Seek them

   _____

3. What must a person do if he expects to see people born into the Kingdom of God? Luke 11:5-9, Isaiah 66:8 _Get up &_
   give what God has given us.

   _____

4. What must the soul winner do in many cases in order to win the unsaved's confidence? 1 Corinthians 9:19-22 _____

Go and meet them where they are on their grounds!

_____

5. What three things must we do before we can see a spiritual harvest? Psalm 126:6 Go out weeping, carrying seed to sow, return with songs of joy

_____

6. What is the seed that is to be sown? Mark 4:14 _____

God's word

7. With what purpose is the soul winner to go forth? Mark 16:15

To preach the good news to all creation

_____

8. For what can the personal worker pray as he goes at his task? Acts 4:29 Boldness

_____

James 1:5 Wisdom

_____

Colossians 4:3 for God to open a door for our message

MAN'S PART IN EVANGELISM (2)

9. What three qualities are to characterize the soul winner's life as he goes forth? Matthew 10:16 _be like sheep among wolves, shrewd as snakes, innocent as doves_

Proverbs 28:1 _Be as bold as a lion_

10. What is the soul winner to urge the sinner to do? 2 Corinthians 5:20 _Be reconciled to God._

11. Where is the soul winner to begin in doing his work of evangelism? Luke 24:47, Acts 1:8 _From Jerusalem to all the ends of the earth_

12. What are we to do with those we help find the Lord? Matthew 28:20, 2 Timothy 2:2 _Teach them to obey everything God has commanded. Teach them_

13. What is on our hands if we fail to do this work of reaching the lost? Ezekiel 3:18 _We will be held accountable for his blood._

APPLYING THE TRUTH

_____

_____

_____

_____

_____

_____

_____

_____

_____

_____

_____

_____

_____

_____

_____

_____

_____

_____

_____

_____

MEMORIZING THE TRUTH – Psalm 126:6, John 9:4

Bible Study Eight

Jesus' Evangelism

INTRODUCING THE TRUTH

After seeing and beginning to apply to your life all that has been studied up to this point, there still remains the question of evangelism pattern.

The pattern of evangelism traditionally practiced by the Church of Jesus Christ is (1) evangelism done almost entirely by pastors and evangelists, (2) evangelism done almost entirely inside of the church building, and (3) evangelism done almost entirely by the method of mass evangelism (commonly referred to as revival meeting).

Is the work of evangelism to be limited to this pattern, or is it to be done by **every believer**, done **everywhere**, and done **all the time**? What pattern did the Lord use? What pattern did He teach? What can we learn from the Lord's life and teachings on this important question and how much of it can be applied to the contemporary situation?

FINDING THE TRUTH

1. The strategy, men, methods, materials, and money used in the work of world evangelization must be adequate to get the gospel to whom? Mark 16:15 _all creation_

   _____

   _____

2. Who was the master soul winner? Luke 19:10 _the_ _Son of Man - Jesus_

   _____

   _____

3. Let's see what we can learn about soul winning from the Lord's life. Analyze the following four situations (given in chronological order) by studying setting (time, place, circumstances), who was influenced, what method He used, and other important observations.

a) Jesus with Nicodemus - John 3:1-21

Setting _____

_____

Person(s) influenced _____

_____

Method used _____

_____

_____

Other observations _____

_____

_____

_____

_____

b) Jesus at Samaria - John 4:4-42

Setting _____

_____

Person(s) influenced _____

_____

Method used _____

_____

_____

JESUS' EVANGELISM

Other observations _____

_____

_____

_____

_____

c) Jesus with adulterous woman - John 8:1-11

Setting _____

_____

Person(s) influenced _____

_____

Method used _____

_____

_____

Other observations _____

_____

_____

_____

_____

d) Jesus at Jericho - Luke 19:1-10

Setting _____

_____

Person(s) influenced _____

_____

Bible Studies for Soul Winners

Method used _____

_____

_____

Other observations _____

_____

_____

_____

_____

4. What can we learn from the sending of the seventy? Luke 10:1-20

_____

_____

_____

_____

_____

_____

_____

_____

5. Where did Jesus indicate that evangelism was to be done in His parable of the great supper? Luke 14:21, 23 _____

_____

_____

6. In summary, what can we learn about evangelism from Jesus' life
   and ministry? _____

   _____

   _____

   _____

   _____

   _____

   _____

   _____

   _____

   _____

   _____

   _____

   _____

   _____

   _____

   _____

   _____

   _____

   _____

APPLYING THE TRUTH

_____

_____

_____

_____

_____

_____

_____

_____

_____

_____

_____

_____

_____

_____

_____

_____

_____

_____

_____

_____

MEMORIZING THE TRUTH – Luke 14:23, John 4:35

The First Century Church's Evangelism

INTRODUCING THE TRUTH

Not only can we learn from studying our Lord's methods of evangelism but we will do well to look at that which was used by the First Century Church.

Did the early Church have the pattern of evangelism which we must adopt today if we are to ever see the gospel taken to every person? What can we learn from the First Century Church that we can apply to the present day?

FINDING THE TRUTH

1. Let us see what we can learn about soul winning from the early Church as recorded in the New Testament. Analyze the following four situations (given in chronological order) by studying setting (time, place, circumstances), who was influenced, what method (personal evangelism, mass evangelism, or both) was used, and other important observations.

   a) Peter and John at Jerusalem - Acts 3:1-4:4

   Setting _____

   _____

   Person(s) influenced _____

   _____

   Method used _____

   _____

   _____

Other observations _____

_____

_____

_____

_____

b) Philip at Samaria and Gaza - Acts 8:5-39

Setting _____

_____

Person(s) influenced _____

_____

Method used _____

_____

_____

Other observations _____

_____

_____

_____

_____

c) Peter at Caesarea - Acts 10:1-48

Setting _____

_____

Person(s) influenced _____

_____

The First Century Church's Evangelism

Method used _____

_____

_____

Other observations _____

_____

_____

_____

_____

d) Paul at Corinth - Acts 18:1-11

Setting _____

_____

Person(s) influenced _____

_____

Method used _____

_____

_____

Other observations _____

_____

_____

_____

_____

2. Who did evangelism in the early Church (just apostles or all followers of the Lord)? Luke 10:1, Acts 8:1-4 _____

_____

_____

3. Where was evangelism done by the early Christians? Mark 16:20, Acts 5:42, 8:4 _____

_____

_____

_____

4. What was the primary means the Lord used in establishing the permanency of His Kingdom? Acts 15:41, 18:22, Revelation 1:4

_____

_____

5. In summary, where are some places where the work of evangelism is to be done as indicated by the pattern set by the early Church? _____

_____

_____

_____

_____

_____

_____

_____

6. What was the evangelism success of the early Church?

Acts 2:36-46 _____

_____

_____

Acts 4:1-4 _____

_____

_____

Acts 17:6 _____

_____

_____

Acts 19:10 _____

_____

_____

1 Thessalonians 1:5-8 _____

_____

_____

7. In your opinion why did they have this success?

_____

_____

_____

_____

_____

_____

APPLYING THE TRUTH

_____

_____

_____

_____

_____

_____

_____

_____

_____

_____

_____

_____

_____

_____

_____

_____

_____

_____

_____

_____

_____

_____

MEMORIZING THE TRUTH – Mark 16:20, Acts 8:4

Conclusion

Because the nature of this series has been self-discovery, the writer has endeavored to say very little. A few concluding statements, however, are made at this time.

Almost 2,000 years ago, God, through the atoning death of His Son, provided a way of salvation from sin for every person.

The Lord Jesus, during His earthly ministry, founded the Church to continue His work on earth after His ascension. To this Church He gave a task—to communicate the gospel to every person in every generation.

To this Church also was given the Holy Spirit to cleanse and empower disciples for this task and to direct them in their work. The Lord Jesus additionally gave a pattern of evangelism. By His life and teachings He outlined that the work of evangelism was to be done by everybody (not just pastors and evangelists), done everywhere (not just at the church building), and done all the time (not just a few seasons out of the year) as the disciples are Spirit-filled and trained.

The early disciples touched the entire civilized world (Acts 17:6) and totally evangelized some portions (Acts 19:10, 1 Thessalonians 1:8) because (1) they meant business about the task, (2) they were filled with the Holy Spirit, (3) they followed the pattern, and (4) the evangelized were soon evangelizing.

Today millions are going to hell every year, the majority because they have never heard the Good News. And every year we're getting further behind in fulfilling the Great Commission. The need of the hour is for the Church of Jesus Christ (1) to see anew her God-given purpose, (2) to experience afresh her God-given power, and (3) to begin to follow her God-given pattern.

May the Lord of the Harvest in these last days raise up men to call and lead the Church back to her New Testament purpose, power, and pattern!

May the office desk, the factory work bench, the home, and a thousand other places become pulpits and every Christian an effective, Spirit-filled evangelist.

Other Helpful Materials from PTWP

I. PERSONAL EVANGELISM MATERIALS

Bible Studies for Soul Winners. Study this book first to get a thorough, biblical understanding of evangelism. Over 30,000 copies in print.
ISBN 1-929451-17-2 • 52 pages $8.95

You can be a Soul Winner – Here's How! Over 60,000 copies of this book hve been used on every continent for over 40 years as a training *how to* manual on personal evangelism.

This book shows you how to –
- Get a vision for the lost
- Live a Spirit-filled life
- Guide any conversation on to the subject of spiritual matters
- Open the Bible and present the gospel
- Actually lead your friend to Christ
- Do door-to-door evangelism
- Do a number of other approaches to evangelism
- Pray for the lost
- Disciple a new Christian
- Multiply until the whole world is reached
- and many other matters pertaining to personal evangelism

Learn how YOU CAN fulfill the Great Commission in this generation.
ISBN 1-929451-13-X • 180 pages $12.95

Special Offer — *You can be a Soul Winner* and *Bible Studies for Soul Winners,* both for $19.95.

The Way to God. A 16-page witnessing booklet you can use to lead your unsaved friends to Jesus. It has been used around the world, on every continent. People have been saved just by reading it. Includes the biblical emphases of repentance and the Lordship of Jesus Christ.
ISBN 1-929451-18-0 . . . .$.25 ea., 10 for $2, 100 for $15

The New Birth—What It Is, and What It Is Not. A 6-page leaflet giving a clear, in-depth presentation of the way of salvation. $.10 ea., 100 for $6.

Prospect Card. Use this card to keep a record of progress with your unsaved prospects. $.03 ea., 50 for $10, 100 for $18.

II. FOLLOW-UP MATERIALS

Basic Bible Studies. A question-and-answer type, foundational Bible study book about the Christian faith. Chapters include:

1. Is There a God?
2. The Issue of Sin
3. What Provision Did God Make for Man's Sin?
4. How Should Man Respond to God's Provision?
5. Abiding in Christ
6. The Christian and God's Word
7. The Christian and Prayer
8. The Christian and the Holy Spirit
9. The Christian and Warfare
10. The Christian and Witnessing
11. The Christian and the Home
12. The Christian and the Church
13. The Christian and Business Affairs
14. The Christian and Discipleship
15. The Christian and Service
16. The Christian and the Return of Christ

ISBN 1-929451-02-4 • 80 pages $11.95

Foundations for the Christian Life by John G. Gill. Written to give the foundation stones for the Christian life, as listed in Hebrews 6:1-3. Many Christians struggle in their Christian life because the proper foundation was not laid in the beginning. This book biblically gives this proper foundation. Questions at the end of each chapter make it even more practical.
ISBN 1-929451-11-3 • 118 pages $11.95

God's Word Puts the Wind in My Sails by Joanne Bachran. A guide to knowing GOD and His Word. It is full of helpful, basic material for all believers, especially new Christians. A reference guide, Bible study, personal devotional, and journal—all rolled into one. A personal compass for a more intimate relationship with God. Very useful!
ISBN 1-929451-08-3 • 216 pages $13.95

III. MATERIALS TO HELP YOU GROW

New Testament Survey Course. A very unique 47-lesson Bible study survey of the New Testament.

- It covers every verse of the New Testament
- It leads you in an in-depth study of each book. You will read the entire New Testament and either answer summarizing questions or summarize the book, a paragraph at a time.
- It harmonizes the Gospels so that you study Jesus' life in a single, chronological narrative.
- It places the letters in the order in which they were actually written.
- This study gives you background information on each book of the New Testament.
- You will apply each book to your own life situation.
- You will decide on verses to memorize from each book.
- You will know the New Testament when you have finished this study!

ISBN 1-929451-03-2 • 234 pages $16.95

Mastering the Word of God—and Letting It Master You! This book is about various methods of in-depth Bible intake: how to hear, read, study, memorize, and meditate on the Word of God. With this book you will learn how to study the Bible. You will be able to develop a life-long plan of in-depth Bible study—mastering God's Word, and letting It master you.

ISBN 1-929451-04-0 • 46 pages $6.95
Workbook • ISBN 1-929451-09-1 • 34 pages $5.95

Bible Outlines. A supplemental book to *Mastering the Word of God.* This book gives an outline for every book of the Bible, a title for every chapter, and other helpful information.

ISBN 1-929451-10-5 • 62 pages $9.95

Getting to Know GOD. A devotional Bible study book on 57 aspects of GOD's Person, Character, and Attributes: His love, His mercy, His faithfulness, His goodness, His glory and majesty, etc. For each attribute, you will read an introduction, prayerfully read three or four pages of appropriate Scripture verses, answer study questions, do research, meditate on and apply the lesson to your life, memorize verses of your choice, and pray a closing prayer. This book was written by an actual Bible study group. This study will change your life!
ISBN 1-929451-05-9 • 288 pages $19.95

Qualities God is Looking for in Us. A 53-week Bible study, devotional book on the qualities God is looking for in us: abiding in Christ, boldness, contentment, diligence, discipline, early riser, forgiving, generous, holy, honest, humble, obedient, praiser, prayer, servant, wise, zealous, etc. For each quality, you will read an introduction, prayerfully read three or four pages of appropriate Scripture verses, answer study questions, do research, meditate on and apply the lesson to your life, memorize verses of your choice, and pray a closing prayer. This book was written by an actual Bible study group. This study will greatly challenge you!
ISBN 1-929451-06-7 • 384 pages $24.95

Preparing the Way Publishers

makes available practical materials
(books, booklets, and audio tapes)
that call the Church to the radical Christianity
described in the Bible.

Some titles include —
The Way to God
Basic Bible Studies
New Testament Survey Course
Mastering the Word of God—and Letting It Master You
Bible Outlines
Getting to Know GOD
Qualities God is Looking for in Us
Bible Studies for Soul Winners
You can be a Soul Winner—Here's How!
The Church Triumphant at the End of the Age
New Wine Skins—the Church in Transition
God's Simple Plan for His Church—a Manual for House Churches
Leadership–Servanthood in the Church as found in the New Testament
Woman—God's Plan not Man's Tradition
Restoring the Vision of the End-times Church
God's Word Puts the Wind in My Sail
Foundations for the Christian Life

For further information, see the PTW web page
at www.PTWPublish.com

Or contact —

Preparing the Way Publishers
2121 Barnes Avenue SE
Salem, OR 97306-1096, USA

phone 503/585-4054
fax 503/375-8401
e-mail <kruppnj@open.org>

ORDER FORM

Preparing the Way Publishers

2121 Barnes Avenue SE, Salem, OR 97306, USA

Voice 503-585-4054 • Fax 503-375-8401

E-mail: kruppnj@open.org • Website: www.PTWpublish.com

PERSONAL EVANGELISM MATERIALS

QTY	TITLE	PRICE	TOTAL
_____	Bible Studies for Soul Winners	$8.95	_____
_____	You can be a Soul Winner—Here's How!	$12.95	_____
_____	Special Offer: Bible Studies/You can be a Soul-Winner	$19.95	_____
_____	The Way to God ....25¢ ea., 10 for $2, 100 for $15.00		_____
_____	The New Birth ....10¢ ea., 100 for $6.00		_____
_____	Prospect Card ....3¢ ea., 50 for $10, 100 for $18.00		_____

FOLLOW-UP MATERIALS

QTY	TITLE	PRICE	TOTAL
_____	Basic Bible Studies	$11.95	_____
_____	Foundations for the Christian Life	$11.95	_____
_____	God's Word Puts the Wind in My Sail	$13.95	_____

MATERIALS TO HELP YOU GROW

QTY	TITLE	PRICE	TOTAL
_____	New Testament Survey Course	$16.95	_____
_____	Mastering the Word of God	$6.95	_____
_____	Workbook	$5.95	_____
_____	Bible Outlines	$9.95	_____
_____	Getting to Know GOD	$19.95	_____
_____	Qualities God is Looking for in Us	$24.95	_____

Ordering Information: Fill in your order and send it **with payment** to Preparing the Way Publishers for processing. A new copy of this Order Form will be included with your order for your future ordering use.

Payments: To avoid extra bookkeeping and handling expenses, credits for less than $1.00 will not be sent. Prices are subject to change without notice. **Full payment is expected with order.**

Postage and Handling for mainland United States orders:

Amount of Order	P & H	Postage and Handling for Alaska, Hawaii,
Under $20.00	$4.00	U.S. possessions, and all other nations:
$20.00 - $39.99	15%	Actual postage charge plus 10% handling
$40.00 and above	10%	

TOTAL Book Order $_____

Plus Postage & Handling $_____

GRAND TOTAL $_____

Ship To:

Name: _____ Date of Order: _____

Address: _____ Telephone: _____

City _____ State _____ Zip _____ Nation _____

Clip and mail

Prayer Request

1. Jamie - teaching negotiations
* 2. Monica's sister and mom - continued healing
* 3. Our church - claim protection, healing, unity, growth, open eyes
* 4. Daycare - full staff devoted to God & love th children, full classes, unity, protection
5. To provide the right place for Elizabeth and I to live in his time - Answered ✓

1. Mom full time job
2. Connie's son - Rick → faith & job
3. Connie's husband - Mike salvation
4. Children's church
5. Smooth moving process
6. Connie & Kris physical strength
7. Jamie's mom & dad - faith

CPSIA information can be obtained at www.ICGtesting.com
Printed in the USA
LVOW08s0302270516

490238LV00001B/82/P